Inspirations in Dough

For Joseph, David and Sophie

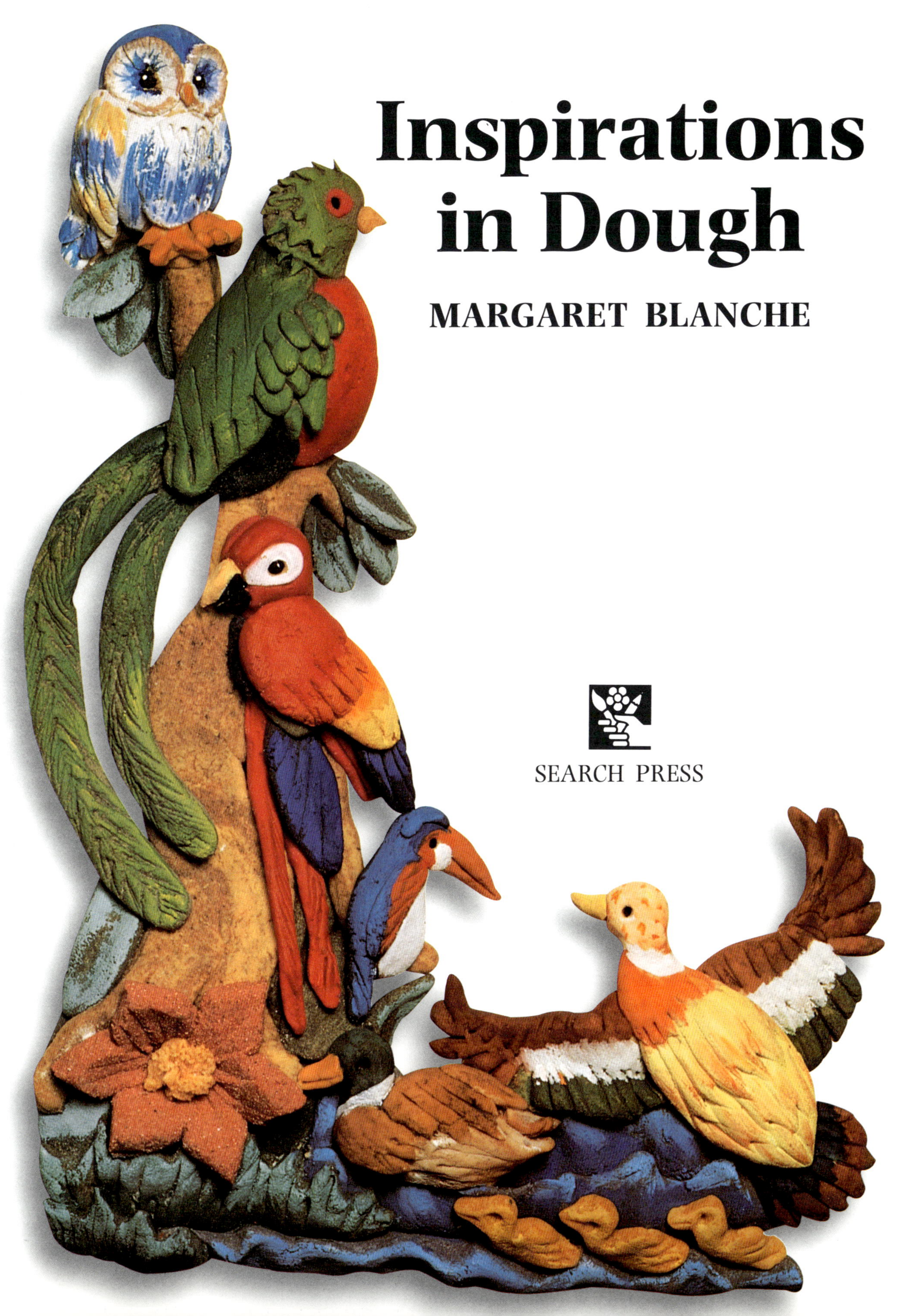

Inspirations
in Dough
MARGARET BLANCHE
SEARCH PRESS

First published in Great Britain 1998

Search Press Limited
Wellwood, North Farm Road,
Tunbridge Wells, Kent TN2 3DR

Text copyright © Margaret Blanche 1998

Photographs by Search Press Studios
Photographs and design copyright © Search Press Ltd.
1998

ISBN 0 85532 837 1

Suppliers

If you have any difficulty in obtaining any of the
materials and equipment mentioned in this book,
then please write for a current list of stockists,
including firms who operate a mail-order service, to
the Publishers:

Search Press Limited, Wellwood,
North Farm Road, Tunbridge Wells,
Kent TN2 3DR, England

Printed in Spain by Elkar S. Coop. Bilbao 48012

*Thanks to Steve for looking after the children, helping
with the chores and putting up with the constant
disruption and mess I have caused.
Thanks also to Lotti, for taking such wonderful pictures
of my work.*

The Owl and the Pussycat

*This stunning three-dimensional model is made in several
stages. The sea is modelled and baked and then the boat is
attached, followed by the pussycat and the owl. The pussycat
is based upon the Pampered cat featured on pages 16–18. The
details such as the money and honey are modelled and baked
separately.*

30cm x 23cm x 18cm deep (12 x 9 x 7in deep)

PAGE 1

Jungle scene

*This model uses a mixture of coloured and natural doughs. The
tree trunk and roots are twisted from yellow dough and the
foliage is added to the base of the model. The animals are then
modelled and attached to the frame. More flowers and leaves
are added to complete the colourful scene.*

33 x 33cm (13 x 13in)

PAGE 3

Tropical birds

*The tree trunk is made from sawdust dough, then the water is
added. The birds are modelled and attached on to the base.
Finally, the flower is modelled from red sand dough and is
attached together with the grass.*

13 x 33cm (5 x 13in)

OPPOSITE

Diplodocus

*This dinosaur is modelled from blue dough, and painted in a
similar way to the stegasaurus featured on pages 14–15. The
folds of skin are made with a knife. After baking, the model is
highlighted with white, green and blue paint.*

8 x 23cm (3 x 9in)

Contents

Introduction

I first discovered salt dough in the early seventies, but I did not take up the craft seriously until two decades later. I had just completed a course in ceramics, and I had a desperate urge to continue being creative. However, I could not afford a kiln . . .

Salt dough is cheap to make, all of the ingredients are easy to obtain, and rather than firing it in a kiln, you only need to dry it out in an oven. Doughcraft is said to have originated in Germany, but it soon became popular all over Europe, and then spread as far as the United States. In Russia and Poland, a biscuit-type recipe has even been developed, which means you can eat unpainted, unvarnished models!

Over the years, I have developed my own special recipe for dough. It is definitely not edible, but it is easy to model with, incredibly versatile, and unlike many other recipes, this unbaked dough keeps for days. I have included a section showing how to make up the dough, and I also give ideas for colouring and texturing it. Modelling the dough is easy with my new recipe, and pieces are attached simply by brushing the joints with water.

I have chosen the subject of animals for this book, and have tried to illustrate how many different ideas it is possible to come up with whilst focusing on one particular theme. There are lots of colourful projects and clear step-by-step photographs will guide you through all the stages needed to make adorable cats, elegant flamingoes, embracing dragons and much more. Most of the models featured can be used as plaques, but at the end of the book I show you how to make free-standing models – this technique takes the craft into a whole new dimension. Unbelievably, the models take no longer to bake than the flat versions.

The special dough recipe that I have developed makes dough an effective modelling medium, and the possibilities are endless. I hope you get lots of inspiration from this book and go on to experiment with other themes such as people, houses, flowers and fruit.

OPPOSITE

Tree of Life

The inspiration for this piece came from the oak tree behind my garden. Once I had decided upon the tree as the basis for the design, I then added the variety of creatures.

35 x 38cm (14 x 15in)

Materials and equipment

All the equipment, materials and ingredients featured in this book are readily available from supermarkets, DIY stores, florists and art and craft shops.

I tend to work with dough that I colour myself using cold water dyes, but you can make the models with natural dough which you can then paint when baked.

I make hangers for many of my models out of plastic-coated garden wire, but you could use string. Alternatively, make a hole in the top of the model, and thread ribbon through.

Most of the items used for texturing can be found around the house or in the garden shed or garage – children's toys or garden netting for example, make excellent patterns, but there are many other items that you could use.

You can embellish your dough with materials such as raffia, seeds, moss or twigs to add realism. Be imaginative and hunt around for alternatives. For instance, you could use dried flowers in place of moss if you are creating a woodland scene.

1. Sieve
2. Kitchen foil
3. Baking parchment
4. Rolling pin
5. Baking tray
6. Cooling rack
7. Water
8. Fork
9. Sharp knife
10. Modelling tools
11. Scissors
12. Sand
13. Sawdust
14. Oil
15. PVA glue
16. Wallpaper paste
17. Salt
18. Flour
19. Mixing bowl
20. Wooden spoon
21. Garden wire
22. Wire cutters
23. White spirit
24. Varnish
25. Paintbrushes
26. Gouache paints
27. Poster paint
28. Palette
29. Cold water dyes
30. Cutters
31. Toy car tyre
32. Garlic press
33. Acorns, dried beans, cloves, seeds
34. Raffia
35. Garden netting
36. Reindeer moss
37. Twigs
38. Four-sided grater
39. Drinking straws
40. Glue gun and glue

Making the dough

I have not given exact quantities of dough for the models featured in this book. You should adjust the quantities given here according to the size of the model you wish you make. This recipe will make a ball of dough approximately 10cm (4in) in diameter.

Cup measurements are given for this recipe. You should use the same size cup throughout and try not to fill it quite to the brim, otherwise you can spill the ingredients. This is particularly important in step 5, as you need to mix wallpaper paste with water in the cup.

No two batches of dough will be identical, as flour often differs very slightly from bag to bag. You can of course vary the proportions of the ingredients to create the consistency of dough you require. You can also experiment with the amount of oil, water and wallpaper paste you add: the more oil you add, the less sticky the dough will be; the less water, the drier and stiffer the dough will be; the more water, the softer; and the thicker the mixture of wallpaper paste used, the longer the dough will keep.

If you want to colour the dough (see pages 12–13), you should introduce the colour to the warm water at step 5, before adding the wallpaper paste.

Recipe

2 cups plain flour

1 cup cooking salt

2 dessertspoons vegetable oil

1 cup warm water

½ cup wallpaper paste

½ cup PVA glue

1 Pour two cups of plain flour into a bowl.

2 Add one cup of cooking salt to the flour.

3 Add two dessertspoons of vegetable oil.

4 Mix with a fork.

5 Pour warm water into a cup. Do not fill right to the brim. Sprinkle approximately half a cup of wallpaper paste into the water and mix with a fork to make a very thick paste. You can add more wallpaper paste or water to adjust the consistency if you wish.

6 Add the wallpaper mixture and half a cup of PVA glue to the flour mixture.

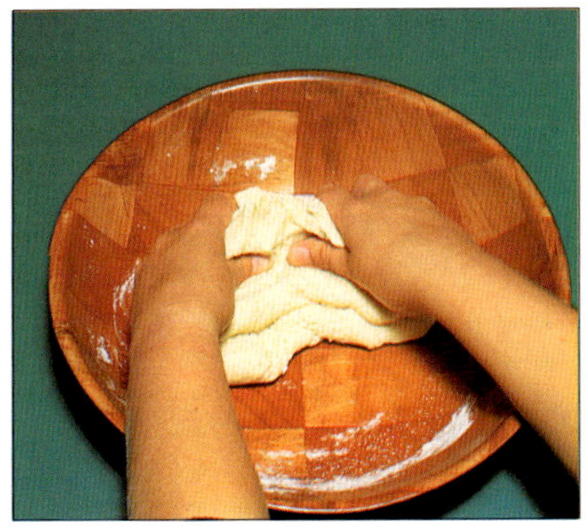

7 Mix with a wooden spoon to begin with and then knead with your hands for about five minutes until the dough leaves the side of the bowl.

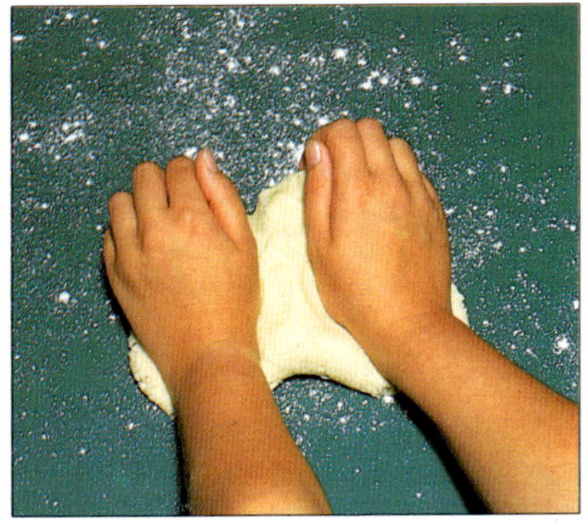

8 Remove the dough from the bowl and knead for a further five minutes on a floured surface until smooth. If the mixture seems a little soft at this point, leave it to stand for an hour and test again. Very often, the dough becomes stiffer. The best time to use the dough is eight hours after making it.

NOTE

If you are working in a very hot environment, the dough may begin to crack. If this does happen, it can be easily rectified by spraying or brushing the dough with water.

Dough can be stored for approximately one week if placed in a plastic bag and kept in a cool place.

If dough has been stored, it should be kneaded well before it is used for modelling.

If stored dough has gone slightly soft, add a little more flour and salt before you model with it.

Colouring and texturing

I like to work with coloured dough as it creates a vibrant effect and makes the painting of the final model much easier. I use cold water dyes to colour the dough but you can use any water-based medium such as gouache, acrylics, powder paints, poster paints or food colouring. The colour should be introduced to the warm water just before the wallpaper paste is added (see step 5, page 11). If powder paint is used, you should add a little more water to compensate for this.

The flower petals on these two pages use different types and colours of dough. You can mix two pre-coloured doughs together. For example, if you have a blue dough and a yellow dough, you can knead these together to produce a green dough. If you mix the doughs together very roughly, you will get a marbled effect.

You can also replace one part flour with different materials such as sawdust, sand, whiting or interior filler to give exciting textures and subtle colours. I use different types of dough to my advantage. For example, I would use a dry, craggy dough for the rough skin of an elephant, or a soft smooth dough for flamingoes or pigs.

The flower centres shown here are made from natural dough which has been textured in different ways, or impressed with various materials such as dried beans, gravel or cloves. Look around your house for objects that you think might make an interesting pattern in the dough – children's toys, kitchen implements and garden tools can often be used. Pressing dough on to the side of a grater creates a lovely orange peel effect, and garden netting, for example, can be impressed on to the dough to give a scaled effect suitable for a dinosaur. I have even taken dough out into the garden and impressed it on to the sides of a tree to get the texture of bark (see the oak tree on page 7). You can use the side of a knife on dough to create the effect of wrinkles in skin, and curved modelling tools are useful for shaping eyelids.

You do not have to use a knife to cut dough – you can use scissors, biscuit cutters or flower cutters (available from cake decorating shops). I sometimes distort a metal cutter to create the shape I require. It is fun to adapt, experiment and get creative!

It is a good idea to keep a record of different coloured doughs, so that you can see how each colour reacts to baking. You could use small motifs such as the flowers on these pages, and you could label the back of each.

PETALS: *Dough made with one part salt, one part flour, one part interior filler*
CENTRE: *Impressed with gravel*

PETALS: *Dough made with one part salt, one part flour and one part sand*
CENTRE: *Impressed with dried beans*

PETALS: *Red and blue dough mixed together*
CENTRE: *Textured with a toy car tyre*

PETALS: *Black dough*
CENTRE: *Dough pressed through a sieve*

PETALS: *Green and yellow marbled dough*
CENTRE: *Textured with a felt-tip pen top*

PETALS: *Red dough mixed with whiting*
CENTRE: *Textured with a fork (pricked)*

PETALS: *Yellow dough*
CENTRE: *Textured with a knife*

PETALS: *Red and yellow marbled dough*
CENTRE: *Textured with a drinking straw*

PETALS: *Green dough mixed with whiting*
CENTRE: *Textured with the tip of a knife*

PETALS: *Dough made with one part salt, one part flour, one part sawdust*
CENTRE: *Textured with a fork (scraped)*

PETALS: *Blue dough*
CENTRE: *Dough pressed through a garlic press*

PETALS: *Green dough*
CENTRE: *Textured with a four-sided grater*

PETALS: *Red dough mixed with yellow dough and whiting*
CENTRE: *Textured with plastic toy bricks*

PETALS: *Dough made with one part salt, one part flour and one part whiting*
CENTRE: *Impressed with cloves*

PETALS: *Blue dough mixed with whiting*
CENTRE: *Textured with garden netting*

Baking, painting and varnishing

Baking

Models should be baked slowly and at a low temperature. Most of the models featured in this book are large and so are baked for a total of five hours: one hour at 100°C (210°F), two hours at 110°C (230°F), and then a final two hours at 130°C (265°F). It is a good idea to turn the oven off for an hour between bakings, and to leave the model inside as it will continue to dry. The model should be removed from the baking tray and placed directly on the oven shelf for the final two hours of baking.

The depth of the dough affects the time of baking required, so if the model is quite thick, you can gouge out some of the part-baked dough from the back to speed up the overall baking time – you should do this just before the final two hours of baking. If you make much smaller models than those featured in this book, you can reduce the baking time. However, you should never bake for less than three hours in total.

You can add baked pieces of dough to unbaked pieces and vice versa. In this way, different sections of a model can be baked at different times before being finally assembled. For example, in this demonstration, the spines of the stegasaurus are baked first to prevent them from sagging when placed on the dinosaur's body.

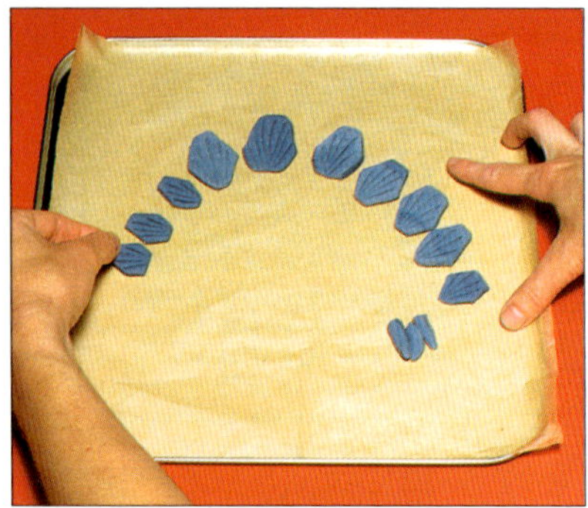

A baking tray is lined with baking parchment and the spines of a stegasaurus are placed on top. The pieces are baked for half an hour at 100°C (210°F) to harden them.

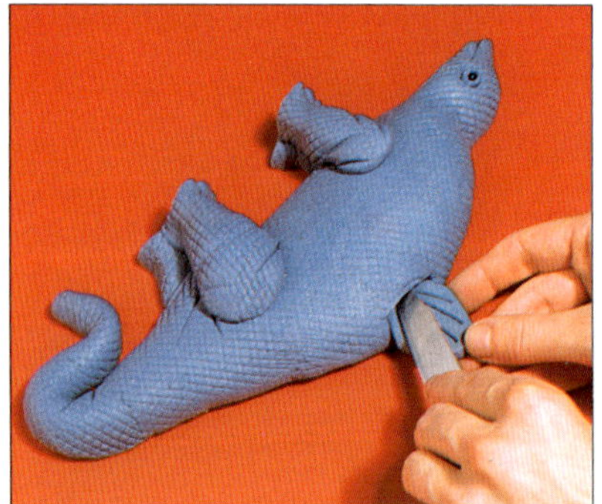

The spines are removed from the oven. The dinosaur is modelled and a knife is used to make a small slit in the middle of the dinosaur's back. A spine is then inserted into the slit.

More spines are added, then the model is placed on a baking tray lined with baking parchment and baked for one hour at 100°C (210°F). The oven is turned up to 110°C (230°F) and the model is baked for a further two hours. The model is then placed directly on the shelf of the oven and baked for a further two hours at 130°C (265°F). The oven is then turned off and the model is left inside to cool down gradually.

Painting

I generally use gouache paint on my models, but you can use any type of water-based paint such as acrylic or poster paints. If you are highlighting a model, it is best to do so whilst it is still slightly warm from the oven, as the paint will dry as it goes on and will therefore not seep into the cracks. If you are applying a wash of paint, you should re-bake the model for ten minutes at 100°C (210°F) to dry the dough out again before varnishing it.

The dinosaur is highlighted whilst it is still slightly warm, to accentuate the texture. Mixtures of white, blue, green and yellow gouache are used. The painting is done carefully, and the surface of the dough is brushed only very lightly.

Varnishing

Varnish protects a model. The best varnish for durability is yacht varnish, as it has a resin in it which will also strengthen the piece. However, you can use any clear spirit-based varnish. Varnish can begin to break down after a year or so. If you do find your models are beginning to look dull, apply another coat.

The model is placed on a cooling rack, with newspaper underneath. It is then varnished with a clear spirit-based varnish. You can use matt, satin or gloss, depending on the finish you want.

Pampered cat

Cats are always popular, so I thought this would be a good model to start with. However, I wanted to create something a bit special – a posh, well pampered cat. I hunted around the house and found an old piece of costume jewellery which I thought I could use to give the collar a little sparkle. Then I decided to sit the cat upon a plush red cushion with rich gold piping to add the finishing touch.

The orange dough used in this project was made by mixing red and yellow dough together, and the salmon colour by mixing a natural dough with the orange dough (see page 12), but you can use paints to achieve these colours. You need a really smooth mix for this model, so make sure the dough is well-kneaded before you begin modelling.

Pampered cat

This cat is really something special. He has beautiful green eyes, a sparkling collar made from a piece of costume jewellery, and whiskers cut from broom bristles. The smart red cushion with its gold piping completes the impression of a truly pampered cat.

20 x 25cm (8 x 10in)

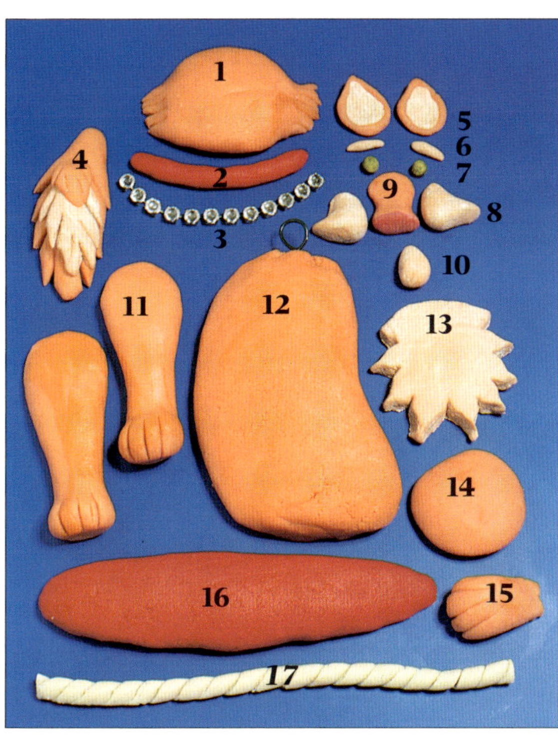

1. Head
2. Collar
3. Jewellery
4. Tail
5. Ears x 2
6. Eyelids x 2
7. Eyes x 2
8. Cheeks x 2
9. Nose
10. Chin
11. Front legs x 2
12. Body
13. Chest
14. Rump
15. Back foot
16. Cushion
17. Cushion piping

All the shapes required to make the cat

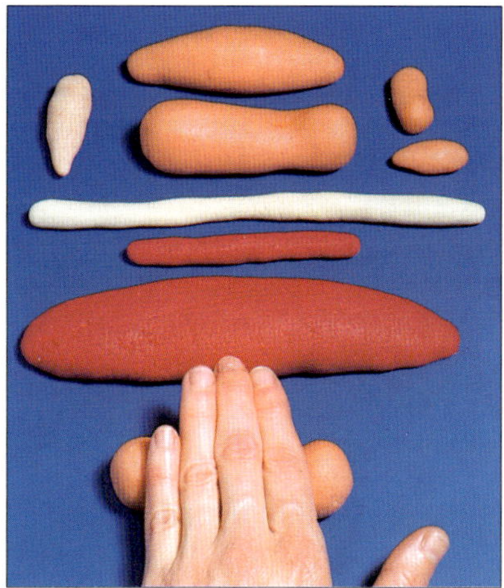

1 Make rolls for the front legs, eyelids, tail, cushion piping, cushion, nose and collar.

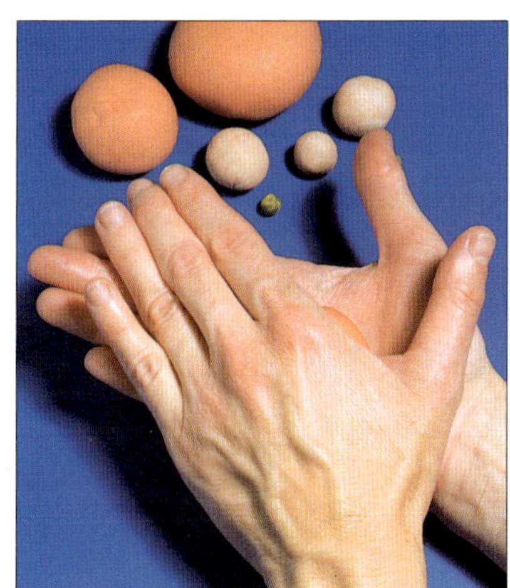

2 Make balls for the head, rump, chest, back foot, chin, cheeks, eyes and ears.

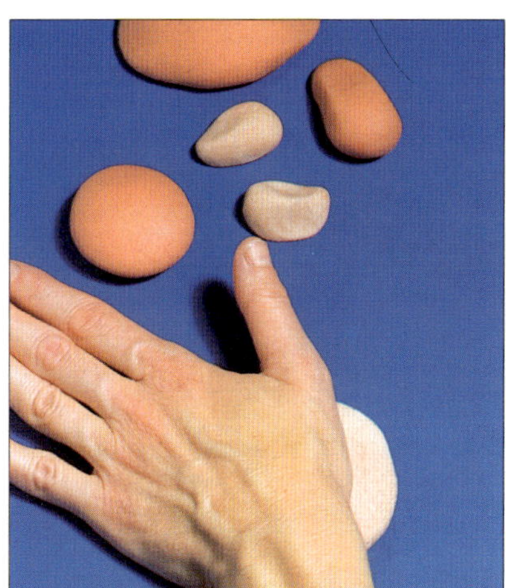

3 Gently flatten and model the shapes with your hands. Cut out the shape of the chest using the tip of a leaf-shaped cutter. Use a knife to add texture to the tail.

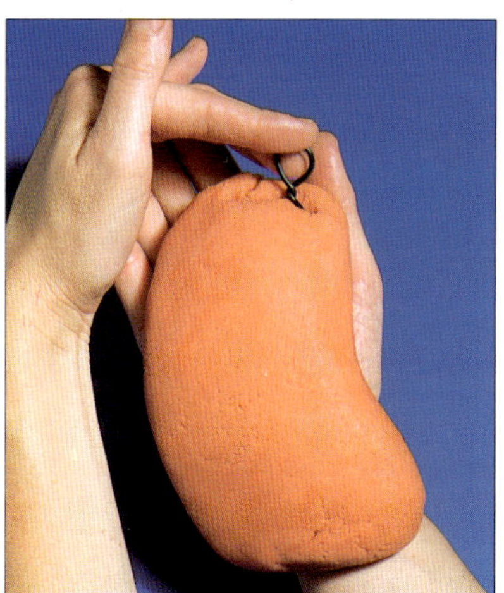

4 Model a large kidney-shaped piece of orange dough to make the body. Twist garden wire to make a hanger, then push it into the top of the body.

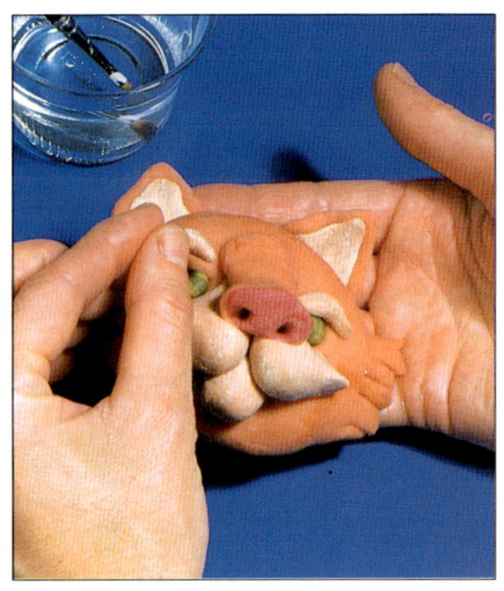

5 Brush all the pieces for the face with a little water and then assemble them.

6 Snip into the sides of the cheeks with scissors to create the impression of fur.

7 Push the tip of a pencil into the muzzle to make small holes. Add fine broom bristles to create whiskers.

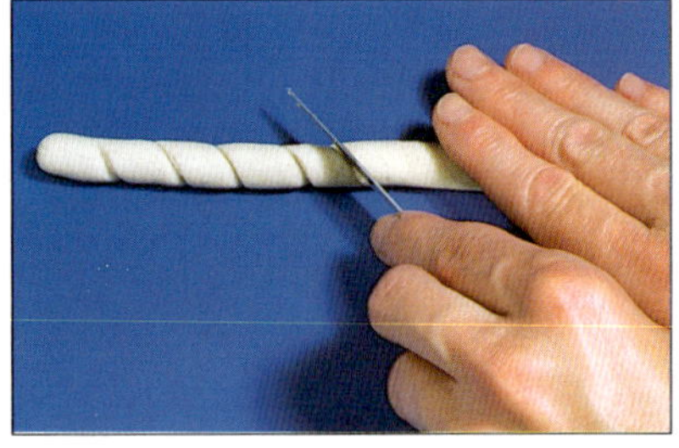

8 Gently roll the piping with one hand and at the same time, carefully cut into it to create texture. Use a sharp knife and hold it at an angle as you work. Attach the piping and the body to the cushion.

9 Attach the head and chest to the body, then add the back foot, rump, front legs, tail, collar and the diamanté jewellery. Use a knife to add the claws to the feet. Bake for five hours (see page 14). Paint the pupils black and add highlights in white. Use gold for the piping on the cushion. Leave the paint to dry before applying varnish.

> **NOTE**
>
> **Attach pieces of dough together by brushing the joints with a little water.**
>
> **Spray the dough with water as you work to keep it moist and to prevent it from cracking.**

Stray cat, lion and tiger

All of the 'cats' on this page are variations on the cat featured on pages 16–18, and all are approximately the same size. They use the same amount of pieces, with slight variations to certain shapes. You could adapt this technique to make a dog. Use a knife to create the impression of fur.

20 x 25cm (8 x 10in)

Wading flamingoes

I used the principle of Yin and Yang as the basis for the composition of this design which has resulted in the shapes of the two flamingoes complementing each other so beautifully. It is important to think of the overall shape of the model when designing a piece from scratch, and not to concentrate solely on the main subject. It is worth roughly sketching out your design before you begin modelling so you can visualise it clearly and make adjustments at that stage.

The pink dough in this project was made by mixing red and natural dough together, and the green by mixing blue and yellow dough (see page 12).

You will need

Dough: blue, pink, green, black, natural

Water-based paint: blue, pink, green, black, white

Paintbrushes for paint and varnish

Scissors

Sharp knife

Leaf-shaped cutter

Rolling pin

Garden wire

Wire cutters

Spirit-based varnish

Wading flamingoes

Yin and Yang is the principal behind this design. The flamingoes are made out of simple shapes, and the wings are textured with scissors. Foliage around the edge of the model frames the scene effectively.

23 x 28cm (9 x 11in)

1 Roll out an oval base from blue dough. Push a twist of garden wire into the back to make a hanger. Mix up a light and dark blue wash then brush it on to the unbaked dough in swirls to suggest water.

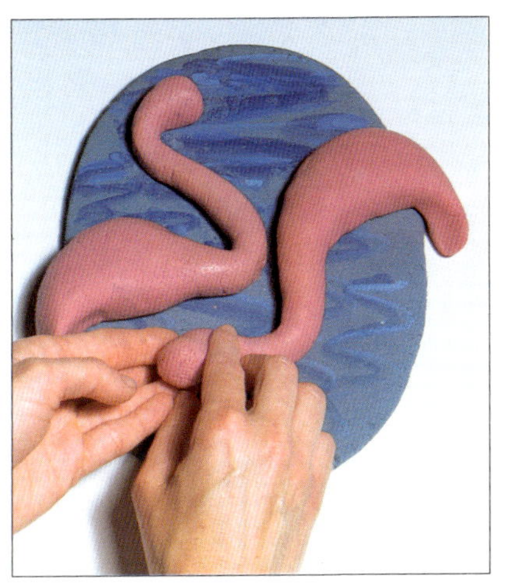

2 Model each flamingo body, neck and head from one piece of dough. Attach both to the blue oval.

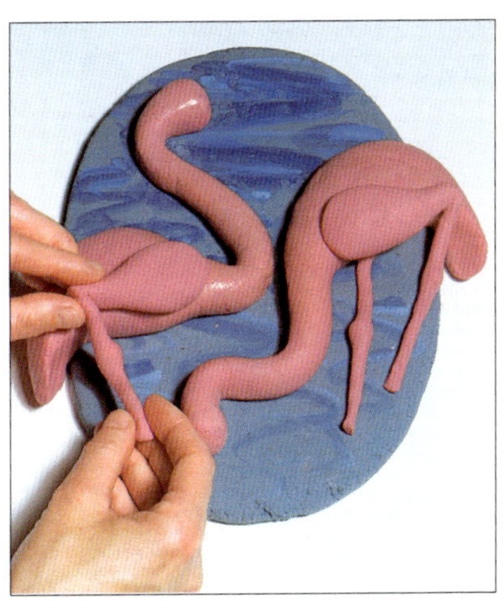

3 Roll the thighs and legs from separate pieces of dough. Attach to the flamingoes.

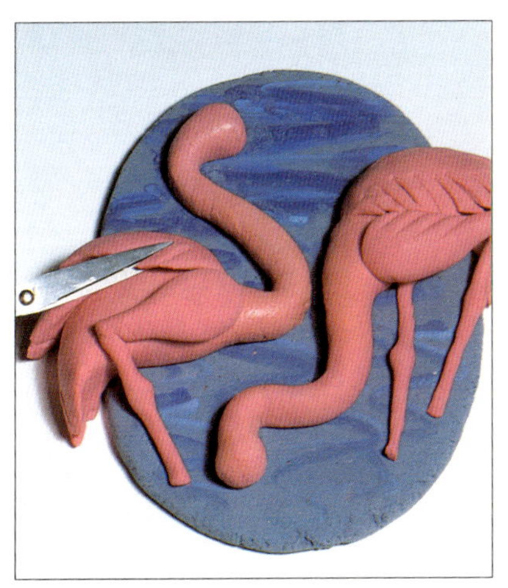

4 Model the wings and attach them to the flamingoes. Use scissors to create feathers on the wings and thighs.

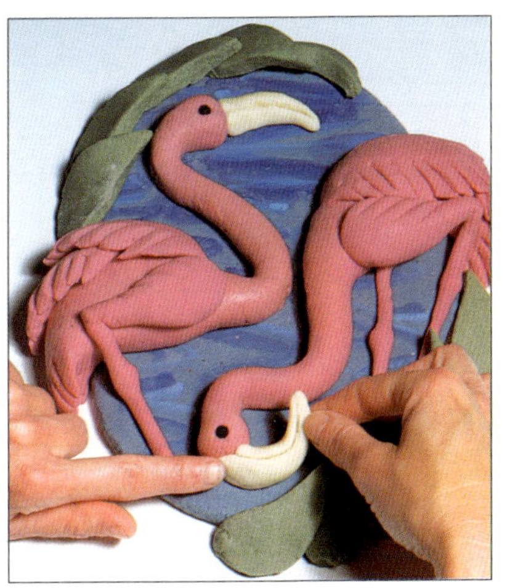

5 Model the beaks from natural dough then score with a knife. Make the eyes from black dough. Roll out green dough, then cut out the leaves from this and shape them. Attach all the pieces to the model. Bake for five hours (see page 14).

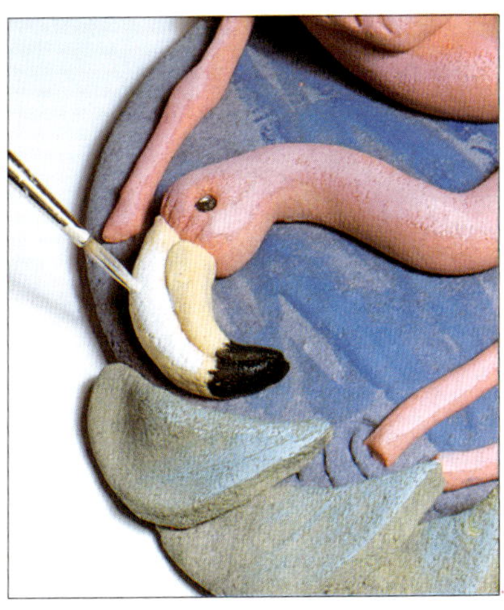

6 Highlight the flamingoes with pale pink and use pale green on the leaves. Paint in the beaks with black and white. Bake for ten minutes at 100°C (210°F) to dry the dough out again. When cool, varnish the model.

Eagle

The wings and body of this impressive eagle are formed out of dark
brown dough; the tail and head are made from natural dough; and
the beak and feet from yellow dough. This model requires only four
hours baking in total. It is then highlighted using orange and light
brown on the feathers, and white on the head and tail.

38 x 15cm (15 x 6in)

Peacock

This peacock has been made entirely from blue dough. The round shapes on the feathers are made by gently pressing my finger into the dough. The colourful circles are painted on after baking, and highlights are added to the peacock's body.

15 x 13cm (6 x 5in)

Parrot

Green dough is used to make this cheerful parrot and the branch is made from sawdust dough (see pages 12–13). The feathers are created by snipping into the dough with scissors. Orange and yellow highlights are added once the model has been baked.

10 x 18cm (4 x 7in)

Woodland deer

This model is a variation on the traditional dough wreath. I used a woodland theme and chose to feature deer, but you could replace them with badgers or rabbits if you prefer. The carpet of greenery on which the deer rest is made using reindeer moss which is available from most florists. You could use dried flowers instead if you wish.

Wreaths take slightly less time to bake than most of the other models featured in this book: this one took four hours in total.

Woodland deer

The doe and her fawn are resting on reindeer moss in this woodland wreath and real acorn cups are used on the oak tree. The wreath itself is made by twisting ropes of marbled sawdust dough together (see pages 12–13).

30 x 30cm (12 x 12in)

24

1 Make a roll of natural dough then coil it around a plate to form a dough ring. Add a hanger made from garden wire. Flatten the dough ring with your fingers. Remove the plate.

2 Roll out green dough to a thickness of about 0.5cm (¼in). Cut out the leaves using a cutter or a sharp knife. Mark in the veins on the leaves using a knife held at a slight angle. Arrange the leaves on the dough ring then attach them.

3 Mix black and sawdust dough together to make a marbled dough (see pages 12–13). Make two rolls and then twist them together. Repeat, to make two tree trunks.

4 Add the tree trunks to the dough ring. Model acorns from natural dough and place them in real acorn cups. Attach them to the tree trunk by pressing them into the dough.

5 Model the mushrooms from red and natural dough, and add them to the dough ring.

6 Model the deer as shown. Use the end of a paintbrush to press the ears into the head. Make the fawn in the same way.

7 Attach the deer to the ring. Place the wreath on a baking tray covered with baking parchment. Position small balls of kitchen foil underneath the ears to prevent them from sagging. Bake for four hours (see page 14).

8 Paint the acorns pale green then highlight them with yellow. Paint white spots on the mushrooms. Paint the deer and the fawn using a light red-brown wash, and use black for their noses. Whilst the paint is still slightly wet, add white spots to the fawn. Bake for ten minutes at 100°C (210°F) to dry the dough out again.

9 Varnish the model. When dry, use a glue gun to apply glue to the base of the wreath, underneath the deer. Press reindeer moss on to the glue.

Stag

The log and the antlers on this stag are made from sawdust dough. The ivy is cut from green dough using a leaf-shaped cutter. Natural dough is used for the fungus, deer and small flowers.

13 x 15cm (5 x 6in)

Fox and vixen

The foxgloves that these foxes are nestling in are made with small balls of purple dough. The end of a paintbrush is inserted into each ball and used to form a bell shape. The foxes are made from natural dough. When baked, they are painted a reddish brown and white highlights are added to the chest and face.

20 x 15cm (8 x 6in)

Farmyard scene

This peaceful country scene is built up on a natural dough base which is then covered with dark and light green dough. The light green dough is made by mixing green dough with natural dough. I wanted to make the model as authentic as possible, so I went out to the garden and gathered twigs which I thought I could use to make the gate bars, and gravel to make a stone wall. Dough is baked at a very low temperature, so it is quite safe to impress the dough with materials such as twigs, and then to bake them.

Farmyard scene

Real twigs form the gate bars in this country scene, and gravel is impressed into natural dough to create the stone wall. Details such as the apple tree and flowers complete this picture of rural tranquillity.

_30 x 23cm (12 x 9in)_

You will need

Dough: light green, dark green, natural, red, yellow, white, black, brown

Water-based: white, yellow, green, black, red, brown

Gravel

Twigs

Sieve

Small flower and leaf-shaped cutters

Garden wire

Wire cutters

Sharp knife

Scissors

Paintbrushes for paint and varnish

Spirit-based varnish

1 Model the hills and the foregrounds from dark green and light green dough. Use natural dough underneath to build up height. Use flower cutters to cut out a few flowers from yellow and white dough then attach them to the middle foreground. Turn the model upside down and snip the edge of the foreground with scissors to suggest grass. Use a knife to add texture.

2 Model the wall from two pieces of natural dough. Push small pieces of gravel into the dough to create a stone effect and add twigs for the gate bars. Push a hanger made from garden wire into the top of each section of stone wall.

3 Make bodies for the sheep using two oval pieces of natural dough. Add black dough for the face and legs. Press natural dough through a sieve to make the sheeps' fleeces. Remove the textured dough from the sieve using a knife, then attach it to the bodies.

4 Model the cow's head from two pieces of natural dough. Add the ears. Use black dough for the eyes, eyelashes and mane and snip them with scissors to texture them. Use the end of a paintbrush to make the nostrils.

5 Attach the sheep and the cow to the background. Model the tree from brown and black marbled dough (see page 12). Cut out the leaves from green dough with a cutter and make the apples from balls of red dough. Attach to the model. Add more flowers then bake for five hours (see page 14).

6 Highlight the sheep with white paint, the leaves with light green, the apples with yellow and green, and the flowers with yellow. Paint the cow with a red-brown. Use white for the muzzle, black for the nose and black, white and yellow for the eyes. Bake for ten minutes at 100°C (210°F). Varnish when cool.

Sow and piglets

This happy family has been modelled so that it looks like the sow and her piglets are lying on real straw. The flat oval base shape is made out of natural dough, then the sow and her piglets are modelled from pink dough. The body and the large back leg of the sow are formed from one piece, and the head and remaining legs are added on to it. The ears, tail and the piglets are then attached. After baking for approximately four hours, the spots are painted on with brown gouache. The model is varnished and then lengths of raffia are stuck on to the base using a glue gun.

23 x 18cm (9 x 7in)

Cuddly panda

The panda is quite a straightforward model to make, although it is comprised of several pieces. I added slightly less water than normal to the white and black dough mixtures to get a rather dry dough. I felt that this would create a suitably rough texture for the fur. I used bamboo to act as a frame to support the panda and make the model more sturdy. The bamboo is made from yellow dough, and the texture is added with a knife. The leaves are made using a cutter, but you could use a knife.

Cuddly panda

This adorable panda is supported by a frame of bamboo. He is made using slightly dry mixtures of black and white dough, to which the texture of fur can easily be added using a knife.

20 x 33cm (8 x 13in)

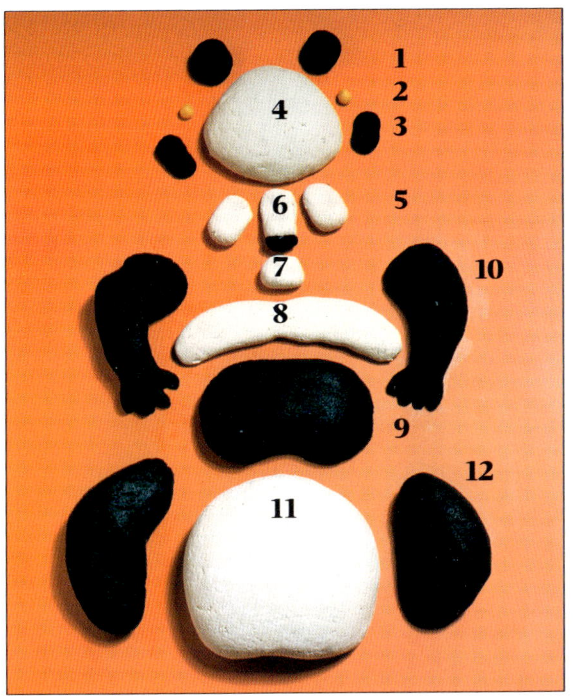

1. Ears x 2
2. Eyes x 2
3. Eye patches x 2
4. Head
5. Cheeks x 2
6. Nose
7. Chin
8. Collar
9. Chest
10. Arms x 2
11. Tummy
12. Legs x 2

All the shapes required to make the panda

1 Model the shapes as shown left, then assemble the panda's head. Assemble the body, then attach the head and the arms to it. Texture the fur with a knife. Insert a hanger made from garden wire into the back of the panda's body.

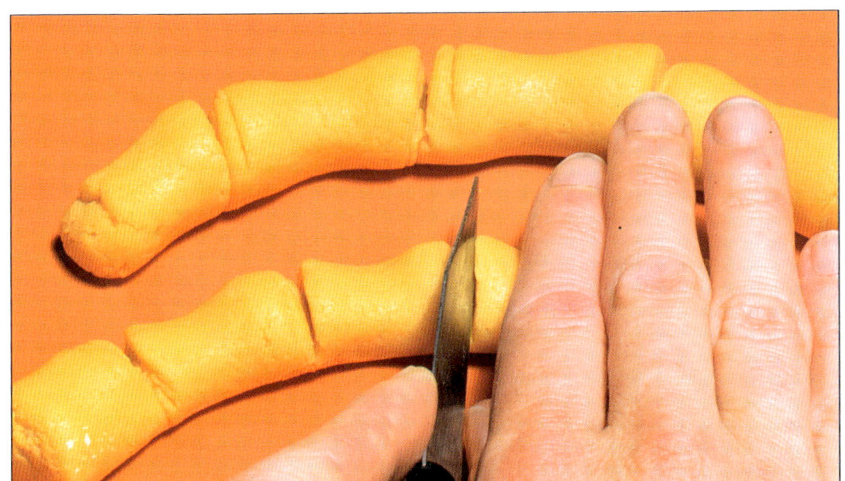

2 Model the bamboo from yellow dough. Roll the bamboo with one hand and at the same time, cut into it with a knife. Attach to the panda. Use a cutter to cut out the leaves from green dough, then score in veins with a knife. Attach to the bamboo. Bake for five hours (see page 14).

3 Highlight the leaves with pale yellow-green, the bamboo with yellow, and the white fur with white. Paint the pupils black then highlight with a dot of white. When the paint is dry, varnish the model.

Elephant

This elephant is made from a dryish black dough and is textured with a knife. After baking, it is highlighted with light grey.

20 x 23cm (8 x 9in)

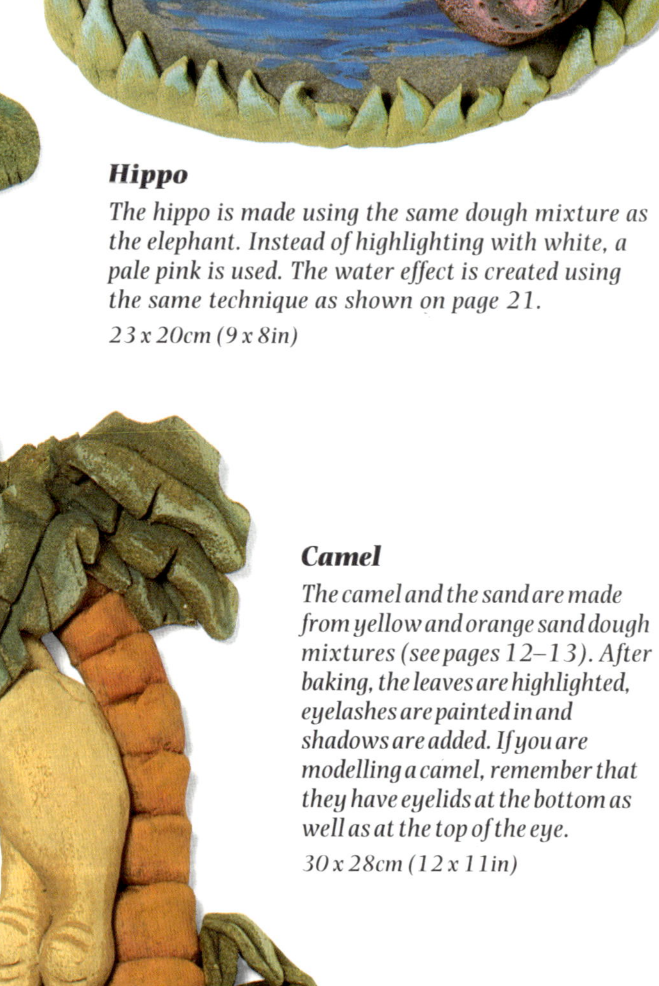

Hippo

The hippo is made using the same dough mixture as the elephant. Instead of highlighting with white, a pale pink is used. The water effect is created using the same technique as shown on page 21.

23 x 20cm (9 x 8in)

Camel

The camel and the sand are made from yellow and orange sand dough mixtures (see pages 12–13). After baking, the leaves are highlighted, eyelashes are painted in and shadows are added. If you are modelling a camel, remember that they have eyelids at the bottom as well as at the top of the eye.

30 x 28cm (12 x 11in)

Giraffe

The tree trunk and this hungry giraffe
are both made from the same yellow
dough. The tree trunk is textured with a
knife, and red-brown markings are
painted on to the giraffe once the model
is baked.

18 x 30cm (7 x 12in)

Romantic dragons

Dragons are often thought of as dangerous, fire-breathing creatures, but I wanted to show them in a different light. The pink and purple dough does a lot to soften their image, and the gold highlights add a touch of extravagance and emphasise the fantasy element.

I needed to construct a frame on which to support the dragons' tails as they are quite flimsy. I decided that fluffy white clouds, highlighted with silver, would be ideal. The bodies and the tails are made separately and they are joined together when attached to the cloud frame. The back legs disguise these joints.

You will need

Dough: white, purple, pink, black

Water-based paint: white, gold, silver

Pointed leaf cutter

Rounded modelling tool or butter knife

Tyre from toy car

Paintbrushes for paint and varnish

Sharp knife

Garden wire

Wire cutters

Spirit-based varnish

Romantic dragons

These adorable dragons are modelled in pink and purple dough and highlighted in gold. The clouds have been included to act as a support and to make the model more sturdy. This design could be adapted to make a very striking picture or mirror frame.

43 x 28cm (17 x 11in)

1 Make balls of white dough for the clouds. Use a knife to add two indents at the top of each cloud, then flatten them slightly. Arrange to form three sides of a rectangle. Insert two hangers made from garden wire into the top of the cloud frame.

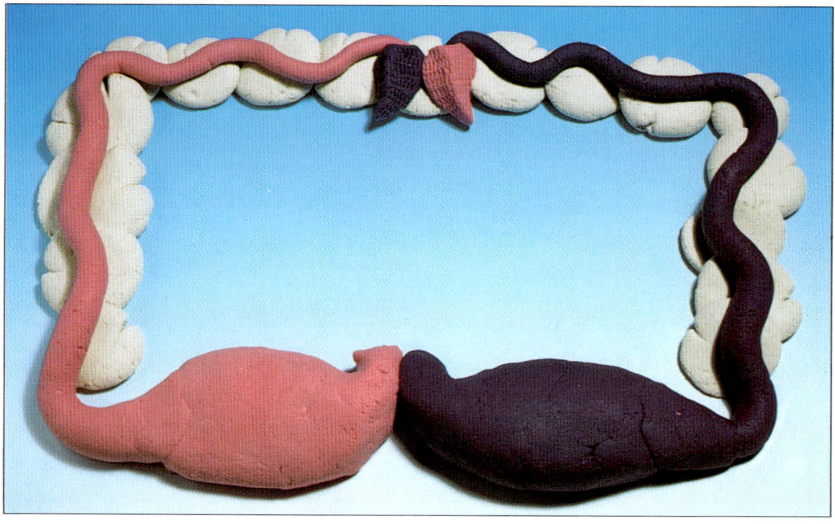

2 Model one dragon body from pink dough, and one from purple. Attach them to the clouds. Roll the tails and mould them to the bodies. Make a pink and purple pyramid to make the tail tips, then texture each with the tyre from a toy car. Attach to the model.

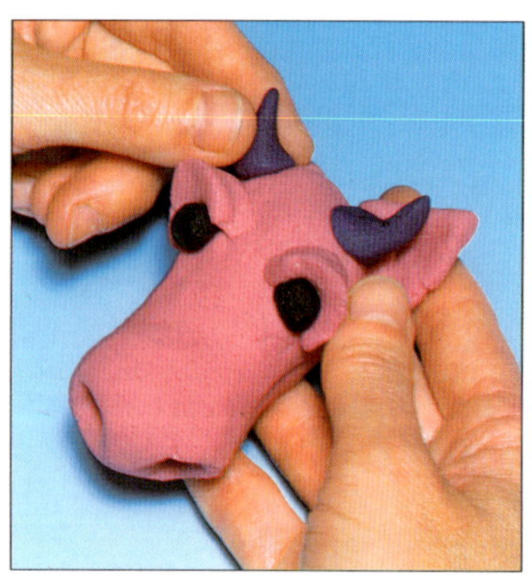

3 Model the heads (see page 30) from pink and purple dough. Add horns in a contrasting colour and use balls of black dough for the eyes.

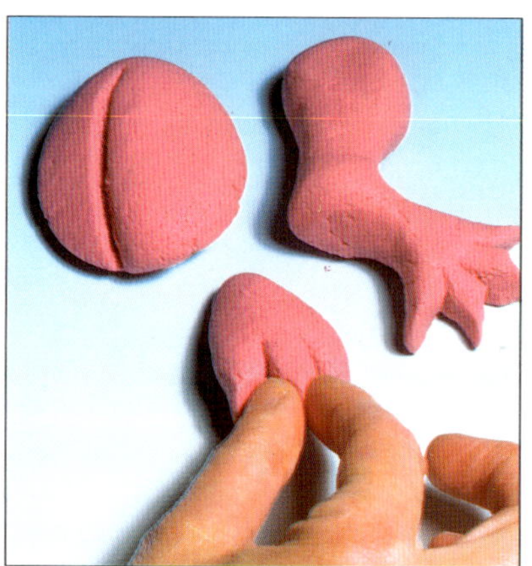

4 Model the back legs and the arms. Cut slits in them with a knife, then pinch with your fingers to form talons. Use a knife to mark a fold of skin in each thigh. Attach all the pieces to the dragons.

5 Cut out flat triangles of pink and purple dough to make the wings. Gently press the side of a paintbrush into the dough to create a fan pattern. Use a round cutter to create the jagged edges. Square off the top of each wing with a knife. Attach them to the dragons.

6 Roll out then flatten a pink and purple strip of dough. Use a pointed leaf cutter to cut zig-zags in each to make the spines (see step 5). Attach to the dragon. Texture the underbelly, the tail and the horns with a knife. Add scales to the body using a rounded modelling tool or a butter knife. Place the model on a baking tray lined with baking parchment and support the wings with balls of kitchen foil to prevent them from sagging. Bake for five hours (see page 14).

7 Highlight the eyes with white, the clouds with silver, and the dragons with gold. When the paint is dry, varnish the model.

Flying dragon

This is a variation on the dragons featured in the project. The same techniques are involved, but no frame is required, and a much smaller tail is used.

33 x 20cm (13 x 8in)

Loveable old bear

The dough recipe that I have developed is far more versatile than the traditional recipe and is perfect for creating three-dimensional models.

The bear in this project uses a sawdust dough (see pages 12–13), which gives a wonderful texture to the fur. The bear is modelled around scrunched up pieces of kitchen foil, which limits the amount of dough you need to use and therefore keeps the baking time down. This technique is very effective, but if you are working on a more complex model than this, you may find that the dough starts to sag as you are working on it. If this happens, simply place the model in the oven for half an hour to harden up the dough.

You will need

Dough: brown sawdust, black, red

Water-based paint: white, silver, gold

Kitchen foil

Rolling pin

Garden wire

Circular cutter

Sieve

Paintbrushes for paint and varnish

Sharp knife

Spirit-based varnish

NOTE
Sawdust dough does not keep as well as other types of dough. It should be used within twenty-four hours of being made.

Loveable old bear

This wise old bear takes no longer to bake than a flat model. It is modelled around scrunched up kitchen foil using a sawdust dough. The waistcoat is made from red dough and the detail is added with gold paint. The spectacles are made from garden wire, which is painted silver.

18 x 20 x 25cm deep (7 x 8 x 10in deep)

1 Scrunch pieces of kitchen
foil into four cylinders for
the arms and legs, and two
rounded shapes for the head
and body.

2 Roll out pieces of brown
sawdust dough for the body,
arms, legs and head.

3 Carefully model two pieces
of flattened dough around
the foil body. Trim and mould
the dough to fit the shape.
Repeat to make the arms, legs
and head.

4 Attach the legs to the body
and firmly fix the head in
position.

5 Model the nose and mouth
from black dough and
attach to the head. Use your
finger to make two holes for the
eyes, then insert small black
balls of dough. Carefully press
them into position.

6 Twist two short lengths of
wire together, shape them
into a semi-circle, then insert
the ends into one side of the
head to form an ear. Make the
other ear in the same way.
Model the ears over the wire
using brown sawdust dough for
the outer ear and black dough
for the inner ear.

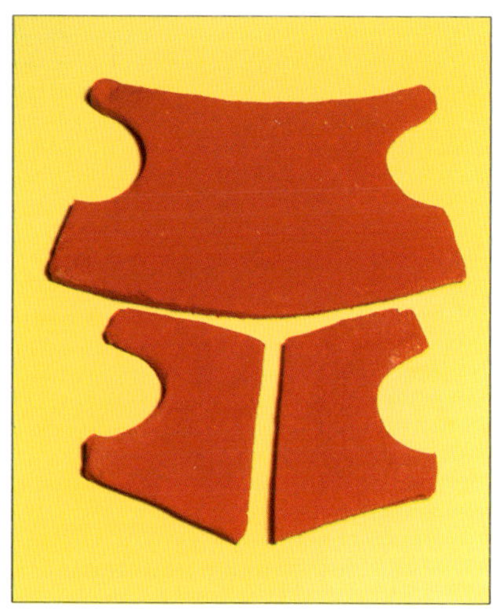

7 Roll out some red dough then use a knife to carefully cut out the three pieces needed to form the waistcoat. Use a circular cutter for the armholes.

8 Press each piece of the waistcoat on to the body. Fold over the collar as you work, then join the pieces together.

9 Position the arms over the waistcoat then attach them in place.

10 Make four circles from black dough to form the pads for the hands and feet. Gently press them into position.

11 Press brown sawdust dough through a sieve. Brush the bear with water, scrape the textured dough off the sieve with a knife, then gently press it all over its body.

12 Model a pair of spectacles from garden wire. Position them over the eyes and push them into the dough. Bake the model for five hours (see page 14). Paint the spectacles silver, highlight the eyes with white, then add gold dots to the waistcoat. When the paint is dry, varnish the model.

Ornamental lion

This lion is made using sand dough (see pages 12–13). He is deliberately left unpainted so as to look like a garden ornament. The face is modelled in a similar way to the cat featured on pages 16–18, but the dough is worked around scrunched up kitchen foil to create the three-dimensional effect.

33 x 15 x 18cm deep (13 x 6 x 7in deep)

Pig

This pig is made from natural dough which is painted after baking, and the long grass, hills and flowers are made with coloured doughs. The long grass is easy to make free-standing: it is modelled, baked, then inserted into a green unbaked dough base. The whole piece is then baked.

15 x 15 x 18cm deep (6 x 6 x 7in deep)

Fang the dog

Fang is made with white, black and pink dough. When baked, the eyes are highlighted with white paint. The kennel is made separately using sawdust dough and the texture of the wood is achieved using a knife. The nails are created by impressing the end of a drinking straw into the dough then painting the holes with silver, once baked.

15 x 25 x 15cm deep (6 x 10 x 6in deep)

FANG
FANG

Dinosaur

This dinosaur is made using a dark green dough. The rough scaly effect on the skin is obtained by pinching the dough. The spines are cut out using a leaf-shaped cutter, a groove is made down the back with a knife and the spines are then inserted (see page 14). A ball of kitchen foil is placed under the head and belly whilst baking to prevent them from sagging. The model is baked for approximately four hours, then highlighted using undiluted yellow gouache.

30 x 13 x 18cm deep (12 x 5 x 7in deep)

Tiger

This stunningly realistic tiger is made using natural dough and all the colour is added with paint after baking. I worked this way because I wanted a very precise shade of orange. However, you could model the tiger from orange dough and then add black stripes and white highlights.

33 x 13 x 15cm deep (13 x 5 x 6in deep)

Index

Red squirrel

This squirrel is made from orange dough that is textured with a knife, and the tree trunk is made from a twist of sawdust dough (see page 25).

15 x 30cm (6 x 12in)